From Zero to AI Creator
A Complete Guide for Beginners Without Any Background in AI

BY
SPENCER RANEY

CONTENTS

INTRODUCTION

Welcome to the World of AI

Welcome to your journey into the fascinating world of Artificial Intelligence (AI)! If you're holding this book in your hands—or reading it on your screen—you've already taken an important step toward understanding and embracing one of the most transformative technologies of our time. Whether you're a student, a professional, a creative, or simply someone curious about AI, this guide is here to show you that anyone, regardless of their technical background, can explore and even create with AI.

Why This Book Exists: Understanding the Rise of AI and Its Importance

Artificial Intelligence isn't just a buzzword or a sci-fi dream anymore—it's a tool that's shaping industries, economies, and even our daily lives. AI powers the recommendations you see on Netflix, helps doctors detect diseases early, assists customer service teams in addressing your queries, and even drives autonomous cars. But despite its ubiquity, many people feel that AI is too complex or intimidating to understand, let alone create.

This book exists to bridge that gap. It's not about turning you into an AI engineer overnight. Instead, it's about making AI approachable, actionable, and empowering for beginners like you. By breaking concepts into manageable pieces, explaining them in plain language, and focusing on hands-on learning, this book will demystify AI and show you that you don't need to be a math wizard or a computer scientist to get started.

AI isn't just for tech companies or researchers—it's for anyone willing to learn and experiment. And by equipping yourself with even a basic understanding of AI, you'll unlock opportunities to innovate, solve problems, and bring your creative ideas to life.

What You'll Learn: A Roadmap of the Skills and Knowledge You'll Gain

Here's what you can expect to gain from this book:

- ➤ **A Clear Understanding of AI Basics:** You'll learn what AI is, how it works, and why it's important.
- ➤ **Familiarity with Key Concepts:** From machine learning to neural networks, we'll explain the building blocks of AI in simple terms.
- ➤ **Practical Skills in AI Development:** You'll gain hands-on experience setting up AI tools, writing basic code, and creating your first AI projects.
- ➤ **Problem-Solving Mindset:** You'll learn how to approach problems with an AI perspective and identify where AI can provide value.
- ➤ **Confidence to Explore Further:** This book is just the starting point. By the end, you'll have the confidence to dive deeper into advanced AI topics, tools, and applications.

By the final chapter, you won't just understand AI—you'll be able to create it, apply it, and continue learning on your own.

Who This Book Is For: Tailored for Absolute Beginners

This book is specifically designed for people with **no prior experience in AI, coding, or technology.** Whether you're a high school student, a stay-at-home parent, an artist, or a professional from a non-technical field, this book is written with you in mind.

You might be asking yourself:

➤ "Can I really understand AI if I don't have a background in math or programming?"
➤ "What if I get stuck? I'm not good with tech."
➤ "Isn't AI too complex for someone like me?"

The answer to all these questions is: **Yes, you can learn AI, and this book will guide you step by step.** We'll start from the very basics and use simple, relatable language to ensure you never feel lost or overwhelmed.

What Is AI? Breaking Down Artificial Intelligence in Simple Terms

At its core, **artificial intelligence** is about teaching machines to mimic human intelligence. It's like giving a computer the ability to "think" or "learn" in a specific way. But don't worry—AI isn't a robot plotting world domination (we'll tackle that myth later).

Here's a simple way to think about AI:

- ➢ Imagine you have a recipe book. If you follow a recipe step by step, you're essentially a computer executing a program.
- ➢ Now imagine if the recipe book could "learn" new recipes based on the ingredients you have in your kitchen—that's AI in action.

AI is used to:

- ➢ **Recognize Patterns:** Like identifying faces in photos or spam emails.
- ➢ **Make Predictions:** Like guessing what movie you might like based on your viewing history.
- ➢ **Automate Tasks:** Like sorting your emails or controlling smart home devices.

It's not magic—it's logic and data combined in creative ways.

Myths About AI: Debunking Common Misconceptions

Before diving deeper, let's clear up some common myths about AI:

Myth: AI is only for tech geniuses.

- ➢ **Reality:** AI tools today are user-friendly, and many platforms require little to no coding knowledge. You don't need a Ph.D. to get started.

Myth: AI will take over all human jobs.

➢ **Reality:** While AI automates repetitive tasks, it also creates new jobs and opportunities, especially for those who know how to use it effectively.

Myth: AI is inherently dangerous.

➢ **Reality:** AI is a tool. Its impact depends on how humans use it. Responsible and ethical AI development is key.

Myth: AI can think and feel like humans.

➢ **Reality:** AI doesn't "feel" or "think" independently. It operates based on data and programming.

Myth: AI is too expensive to learn or create.

➢ **Reality:** Many free resources, tools, and platforms exist for beginners. You don't need a huge budget to explore AI.

How to Get the Most Out of This Book: Actionable Tips to Stay Motivated and Engaged

Learning something new can be challenging, but with the right approach, it can also be incredibly rewarding. Here are some tips to help you make the most of this book:

1. Embrace a Beginner's Mindset

> It's okay not to know everything at first. Focus on learning step by step.
> Don't be afraid to ask questions, even if they seem "basic."

2. Practice What You Learn

> Theory alone won't help you master AI. Take time to complete the exercises and hands-on projects in this book.
> Experiment and make mistakes—trial and error is part of the process.

3. Stay Consistent

> Set aside dedicated time for learning AI, even if it's just 20 minutes a day.
> Break chapters into manageable sections to avoid feeling overwhelmed.

4. Leverage Community Support

> Join online forums, social media groups, or local meetups for AI beginners.
> Share your progress, ask for help, and learn from others.

5. Keep an Open Mind

> AI is a rapidly evolving field. Stay curious and flexible as you learn.
> Don't hesitate to explore new tools, techniques, and concepts beyond this book.

Congratulations on taking your first step toward becoming an AI creator! By the end of this journey, you'll look back and see just how far you've come. So, let's get started and dive into the exciting world of AI!

Part 1: Understanding the Basics of AI

Chapter 01

What Is AI and Why It Matters

Artificial Intelligence (AI) is a term that sparks both curiosity and confusion. To some, it's a revolutionary force transforming industries, and to others, it's an intimidating concept associated with complex algorithms and robots. This chapter will break down the basics of AI in simple, relatable terms, explore its real-world applications, and help you understand why it's so important. By the end of this chapter, you'll see AI as an accessible and transformative tool that anyone, including you, can learn to work with.

The Definition of AI: Simple Examples to Explain What AI Is

At its core, Artificial Intelligence is the ability of machines to mimic human intelligence. This doesn't mean machines can think or feel like humans, but it does mean they can perform tasks that typically require human intelligence, such as recognizing speech, making decisions, or solving problems.

Think of AI as teaching a computer to "act smart." Here's a simple analogy:

➢ Imagine you're teaching a child how to recognize animals. You show them pictures of dogs and cats and explain the differences. Over time, the child learns to identify dogs and cats on their own.
➢ Now replace the child with a computer and the pictures with data. The process of training the computer to recognize patterns in the data is what we call AI.

Simple Examples of AI

> **Virtual Assistants:** AI like Siri or Alexa can understand your voice commands and perform tasks such as setting reminders or playing music.
> **Spam Filters:** Your email service uses AI to distinguish between important emails and spam.
> **Navigation Systems:** Apps like Google Maps use AI to find the fastest routes and predict traffic conditions.

These are not futuristic ideas—they're examples of AI you probably encounter every day.

Types of AI: Narrow AI vs. General AI in Everyday Life

Not all AI is created equal. It's important to distinguish between the different types of AI to understand its capabilities and limitations.

1. Narrow AI (Weak AI)

> **Definition:** Narrow AI is designed to perform a specific task or a set of closely related tasks. It doesn't "think" beyond its programming.
> **Examples in Everyday Life:**
> **Recommendation Systems:** Netflix suggesting movies you might like based on your viewing history.
> **Chatbots:** Automated customer service tools that can answer basic queries.
> **Facial Recognition:** Used to unlock smartphones or identify people in photos.

> **Key Point:** Narrow AI is everywhere. It's powerful but limited to what it's trained to do.

2. General AI (Strong AI)

> **Definition:** General AI refers to machines that can perform any intellectual task a human can do, with the ability to reason, learn, and adapt across a wide range of activities.
> **Current Status:** General AI is still theoretical. While it's a popular topic in movies, it doesn't exist yet in reality.
> **Why It Matters:** Understanding the difference between narrow and general AI helps you focus on practical, real-world AI applications rather than getting lost in science fiction.

Where You Encounter AI Daily: From Chatbots to Recommendation Systems

AI is integrated into many aspects of our daily lives, often in ways we don't even notice. Let's explore some of the most common examples:

1. Chatbots and Virtual Assistants

> Virtual assistants like Google Assistant and Amazon Alexa use AI to understand your commands and provide relevant responses.
> Chatbots on websites can answer customer queries, saving time and improving user experience.

2. Recommendation Systems

- Streaming platforms like Spotify and Netflix analyze your preferences to suggest songs, movies, or shows you're likely to enjoy.
- E-commerce platforms like Amazon recommend products based on your browsing and purchasing history.

3. Healthcare Applications

- AI-powered tools help doctors analyze medical images, predict diseases, and personalize treatments for patients.

4. Smart Devices

- AI is at the heart of smart home devices like thermostats, security cameras, and voice-controlled lighting systems.

5. Social Media

- Platforms like Facebook and Instagram use AI to curate your feed, detect harmful content, and target ads.

Understanding where AI appears in your life can help you see its practical value and inspire ideas for how you might create similar tools.

How AI Impacts Society: Healthcare, Education, Business, and Beyond

AI isn't just a convenience—it's a transformative force shaping industries and society. Let's explore some key areas where AI is making an impact:

1. Healthcare

- ➤ **Early Diagnosis:** AI tools analyze medical data to identify diseases like cancer at earlier stages.
- ➤ **Drug Discovery:** AI accelerates the process of developing new medications.
- ➤ **Personalized Medicine:** AI helps tailor treatments to individual patients based on their unique genetic and health profiles.

2. Education

- ➤ **Personalized Learning:** AI-driven platforms adjust lessons and exercises based on each student's pace and performance.
- ➤ **Accessibility:** AI creates tools like speech-to-text and translation software, breaking down barriers for students with disabilities or language challenges.

3. Business

- ➤ **Automation:** AI handles repetitive tasks like data entry, freeing employees to focus on more creative work.
- ➤ **Customer Insights:** AI analyzes consumer data to predict trends and improve marketing strategies.

4. Environment

➤ **Climate Predictions:** AI models predict weather patterns and natural disasters to improve preparedness.
➤ **Sustainability:** AI optimizes energy consumption and monitors pollution levels to protect the planet.

These examples illustrate why AI is not just a technical advancement—it's a tool for solving global challenges.

The Ethics of AI: Why Fairness, Privacy, and Accountability Matter

As powerful as AI is, it's not without challenges. Ethical considerations are critical to ensure AI benefits everyone fairly.

1. Fairness

➤ **The Problem:** AI systems can inherit biases from the data they're trained on, leading to unfair outcomes.
➤ **Example:** An AI hiring tool might unintentionally favor one demographic over another.
➤ **The Solution:** Developers must actively identify and reduce bias in their systems.

2. Privacy

➤ **The Problem:** AI often relies on large amounts of personal data, raising concerns about how this data is used and stored.
➤ **Example:** Social media platforms using AI to target ads may compromise user privacy.

> **The Solution:** Transparent data policies and user consent are essential.

3. Accountability

> **The Problem:** When AI makes decisions, who is responsible if something goes wrong?
> **Example:** If a self-driving car causes an accident, determining liability is complex.
> **The Solution:** Clear regulations and accountability frameworks are needed.

Understanding these ethical challenges will help you think critically about how to use AI responsibly.

Your AI Learning Journey: Setting Realistic Expectations and Goals

Embarking on your AI journey can feel overwhelming, but it doesn't have to be. Setting realistic expectations and clear goals will keep you motivated and on track.

1. Start Small

> Focus on learning basic concepts and tools before diving into advanced topics.
> Your first project doesn't have to be groundbreaking—it's about building confidence.

2. Embrace Mistakes

> Learning AI is a process of trial and error. Mistakes are opportunities to grow.

3. Define Your Goals

➤ Do you want to understand AI concepts, build simple projects, or explore career opportunities? Tailor your learning to your goals.

4. Commit to Consistency

➤ Dedicate regular time to learning, whether it's 15 minutes a day or a few hours a week.

5. Celebrate Progress

➤ Every concept you understand and every project you complete is a milestone worth celebrating.

By setting the right expectations and staying focused, you'll be amazed at how much you can achieve.

Artificial Intelligence is not just for experts or tech enthusiasts—it's for anyone curious and willing to learn. By understanding what AI is, where it fits into daily life, and why it matters, you're already well on your way to becoming an AI creator. Let's continue this journey together!

Chapter 02

The Key Building Blocks of AI

AI is like a high-performing machine, but like any machine, it doesn't run without its essential parts. In this chapter, we'll break down the key building blocks that make AI work, explain the concepts in an easy-to-understand way, and introduce you to the tools and technologies that will enable you to take your first steps in AI creation. By the end of this chapter, you'll understand what makes AI tick and how to set up a beginner-friendly environment to start your journey.

Data: The Fuel for AI

Just as cars need fuel to run, AI systems need data to function. Data is the lifeblood of AI—it's what enables machines to learn, improve, and make decisions.

1. Why Data Is Essential

AI learns from examples, and data provides those examples. For instance:

➢ To teach AI to recognize cats in photos, you'd need to feed it thousands of images of cats.
➢ The more high-quality data you provide, the better the AI's performance will be.

2. Where Does Data Come From?

Data comes from a variety of sources, including:

➢ **User Data:** Information collected from apps, websites, and social media.
➢ **Sensors:** Data from devices like cameras, microphones, or IoT sensors.

> **Public Datasets:** Open data repositories like Kaggle or Google Dataset Search offer free data for learning.

3. Characteristics of Good Data

Not all data is created equal. For AI to work effectively, the data must be:

> **Relevant:** It should match the task you want the AI to perform.
> **Accurate:** Errors in data lead to poor AI predictions.
> **Diverse:** A variety of examples ensures the AI doesn't become biased.

Algorithms Explained Simply: Demystifying How AI "Thinks"

While data is the fuel for AI, algorithms are the engines. They define how the AI processes the data and learns from it.

1. What Is an Algorithm?

An algorithm is simply a set of rules or instructions that tells a computer what to do. Think of it as a recipe:

> The ingredients are the data.
> The recipe steps are the algorithm.
> The final dish is the AI's prediction or output.

2. How Do AI Algorithms Work?

AI algorithms identify patterns in data and use those patterns to make predictions. For example:

➢ A weather prediction algorithm might analyze past weather data to forecast tomorrow's temperature.
➢ A recommendation algorithm might study your viewing history to suggest movies you might enjoy.

3. Key Algorithms in AI

There are many algorithms, but here are a few beginner-friendly examples:

➢ **Decision Trees:** Like a flowchart that asks yes/no questions to make a decision.
➢ **Linear Regression:** Predicts values, such as estimating house prices based on size.
➢ **Clustering:** Groups similar items, like categorizing emails into folders.

Machine Learning vs. Deep Learning: Breaking Down These Key Concepts

You've likely heard the terms **Machine Learning (ML)** and **Deep Learning (DL)** used interchangeably, but they're not the same. Let's clarify the difference.

1. Machine Learning (ML)

➢ **Definition:** ML is a subset of AI that enables machines to learn from data without being explicitly programmed.

- ➢ **How It Works:** Algorithms analyze data, find patterns, and make predictions.
- ➢ **Example:** Spam filters learn to recognize spam emails based on past examples.

2. Deep Learning (DL)

- ➢ **Definition:** DL is a more advanced subset of ML that uses artificial neural networks, inspired by the human brain, to process large datasets.
- ➢ **How It Works:** Deep learning models have multiple "layers" of neurons that progressively refine the data to improve accuracy.
- ➢ **Example:** Image recognition systems use DL to identify objects in photos.

3. Key Differences

- ➢ ML works well with smaller datasets and simpler problems, while DL shines when handling massive datasets and complex tasks like image or speech recognition.
- ➢ DL requires more computational power and time compared to ML.

AI Tools and Technologies: A Brief Introduction to Python, TensorFlow, and Others

To build AI, you need tools and technologies that simplify the process. Luckily, many beginner-friendly tools exist today.

1. Python: The Language of AI

➤ **Why Python?** Python is widely used in AI because it's simple, versatile, and has a rich ecosystem of libraries for AI development.
➤ **Examples of Python Libraries:**

✓ **NumPy:** For numerical calculations.
✓ **Pandas:** For working with datasets.
✓ **Matplotlib:** For visualizing data.

2. TensorFlow and PyTorch: Powerhouses of AI Development

➤ These are frameworks for building and training machine learning and deep learning models.
➤ TensorFlow is great for beginners due to its extensive documentation and community support.
➤ PyTorch is preferred for its simplicity and flexibility in experimentation.

3. Jupyter Notebook: Your Workspace

➤ A Jupyter Notebook is an interactive environment where you can write and run Python code.
➤ It's perfect for learning AI because it allows you to combine code, text, and visuals in one place.

Examples of AI in Action: Visuals and Scenarios to Make It Relatable

Understanding AI concepts becomes easier when you see them in action. Let's look at a few relatable examples:

1. Virtual Assistants

➢ AI algorithms process your voice, convert it into text, and respond intelligently.
➢ Example: Asking Siri, "What's the weather like today?"

2. Image Recognition

➢ AI scans images to identify objects, people, or scenes.
➢ Example: Google Photos grouping pictures of your friends using facial recognition.

3. Online Shopping Recommendations

➢ AI analyzes your browsing and purchase history to suggest products.
➢ Example: Amazon recommending a phone case after you purchase a new smartphone.

4. Fraud Detection

➢ AI monitors banking transactions for unusual activity.
➢ Example: Your bank flags a suspicious transaction and alerts you.

These examples show how AI touches almost every aspect of our lives, often behind the scenes.

Your First Step: Setting Up a Beginner-Friendly AI Environment

Now that you understand the basics, it's time to take action. Setting up your AI environment is the first step toward hands-on learning.

1. Install Python

➢ Download Python from python.org. Choose the latest stable version for your operating system.

2. Set Up Jupyter Notebook

➢ Install Jupyter Notebook by running the following command in your terminal or command prompt:

```
pip install notebook
```

Launch Jupyter Notebook by typing:

```
jupyter notebook
```

3. Install AI Libraries

Use Python's package manager (pip) to install essential libraries:

```
pip install numpy pandas matplotlib tensorflow
```

4. Explore Pre-Built Datasets

➢ Visit platforms like Kaggle or Google Dataset Search to download free datasets for practice.

5. Write Your First Program

➤ Open Jupyter Notebook and write a simple Python program to ensure everything works:

```
print("Hello, AI World!")
```

6. Stay Organized

➤ Create a dedicated folder on your computer for all your AI projects and learning materials.

By setting up this environment, you're ready to dive into hands-on AI projects in the upcoming chapters.

Understanding these key building blocks of AI lays the foundation for your learning journey. From data to algorithms, tools to practical examples, you're now equipped with the knowledge to move forward with confidence. Let's keep building on this momentum as we dive deeper into the world of AI in the next chapter!

Part 2: Getting Hands-On with AI

Chapter 03

Setting Up Your AI Workspace

Now that you've learned the fundamentals of AI, it's time to get hands-on. In this chapter, you'll set up your AI workspace—the digital environment where you'll build, experiment with, and refine AI projects. Whether you're using a personal computer or relying on cloud tools, this chapter will guide you step-by-step. By the end, you'll have a fully functional setup tailored to your needs, ready to bring your AI ideas to life.

Choosing Your Tools: Free vs. Paid Software and Platforms

The first step in creating your AI workspace is deciding which tools and platforms to use. Luckily, the world of AI offers plenty of free options, so you don't have to spend a dime to get started.

1. Free Tools

Free tools are perfect for beginners and hobbyists. Here are some commonly used ones:

➢ **Python:** The go-to programming language for AI, free to download and use.
➢ **Google Colab:** A free, cloud-based platform where you can run Python code without requiring a powerful computer.
➢ **scikit-learn, TensorFlow, and PyTorch:** Popular free libraries for building AI models.

2. Paid Tools

If you want more advanced features or support, paid tools might be worth considering:

➢ **MATLAB:** A premium tool for numerical computing, often used in academia and industry.
➢ **AutoML Platforms:** Tools like Google Cloud AutoML and Amazon SageMaker simplify AI model creation but come with subscription fees.
➢ **Data Storage Services:** If you're working with large datasets, you may need to pay for cloud storage like Google Drive or AWS S3.

3. Which Should You Choose?

➢ **If you're a beginner:** Stick to free tools like Python and Google Colab.
➢ **If you're pursuing advanced or professional projects:** Consider investing in paid tools once you're more experienced.

Installing Python: Step-by-Step Instructions for Beginners

Python is the foundation of most AI projects. Follow these steps to get it up and running on your computer.

1. Download Python

➢ Visit the official Python website: python.org.
➢ Click on the "Downloads" section and select the version compatible with your operating system (Windows, macOS, or Linux).

2. Install Python

> ➤ Run the downloaded installer.
> ➤ **Important:** During installation, check the box that says "Add Python to PATH." This will make it easier to run Python from your command line.

3. Verify Installation

> ➤ Open your command prompt (Windows) or terminal (macOS/Linux).

```
python --version
```

> ➤ If installed correctly, it will display the version of Python you installed.

4. Install pip (Python Package Manager)

Pip is a tool that allows you to install additional libraries needed for AI. It typically comes with Python, but you can verify it with:

```
pip --version
```

If pip isn't installed, follow the instructions on the Python website to install it.

AI Frameworks Simplified: TensorFlow, PyTorch, and scikit-learn for Starters

AI frameworks are libraries that make building AI models easier by providing pre-built tools and functions. Let's introduce three beginner-friendly frameworks:

1. TensorFlow

➤ **What It's For:** Building machine learning and deep learning models.
➤ **Why Use It:** TensorFlow is well-documented and widely used, making it beginner-friendly.

How to Install:

```
pip install tensorflow
```

2. PyTorch

➤ **What It's For:** Flexible and dynamic AI development, often preferred for research.
➤ **Why Use It:** PyTorch's simplicity makes it easy to experiment with new ideas.

How to Install

```
pip install torch torchvision
```

3. scikit-learn

➤ **What It's For:** Simplifying machine learning tasks like classification and regression.
➤ **Why Use It:** It's perfect for beginners and works seamlessly with Python's data analysis libraries.

How to Install:

```
pip install scikit-learn
```

Using Google Colab: How to Work on AI Without Needing a Powerful Computer

AI projects can demand significant computing power, but don't worry — Google Colab has you covered. This free, cloud-based platform allows you to run Python code in a browser without straining your computer's resources.

1. What Is Google Colab?

➤ Google Colab is an online environment for running Jupyter Notebooks.
➤ It's especially useful if your computer has limited processing power or memory.

2. Setting Up Google Colab

➤ Visit colab.research.google.com.
➤ Log in with your Google account.
➤ Create a new notebook by clicking **File > New Notebook.**

3. Why Google Colab Is Great for Beginners

➤ **Free Access to GPUs/TPUs:** These accelerators make training AI models faster.
➤ **Pre-Installed Libraries:** Popular AI libraries like TensorFlow and PyTorch are already installed.
➤ **No Installation Hassle:** You don't need to configure anything on your computer.

4. Running Your First Code

➤ In the first cell, type the following and hit **Shift + Enter**

```
print("Hello, AI World!")
```

Organizing Your Projects: Best Practices for Naming, Versioning, and Saving Files

A well-organized workspace is crucial as you begin working on AI projects. Here are some tips to keep things neat and efficient:

1. Naming Conventions

➤ Use clear and descriptive names for files and folders.

○ Example: Instead of `project1.py`, use `image_classification_project.py`.

➤ Avoid spaces in file names; use underscores (_) or hyphens (-) instead.

2. Version Control

➤ Save different versions of your projects as you make progress.

Example: `image_project_v1.py`, `image_project_v2.py`.

➤ Use tools like Git and GitHub for version control once you're comfortable.

3. Folder Structure

➢ Keep your files organized with a clear folder structure

AI Projects/

   Project Name/

      data/

      scripts/

      models/

      results/

4. Regular Backups

➢ Use cloud storage like Google Drive or Dropbox to back up your work.

Troubleshooting Basics: Common Errors and How to Fix Them

Mistakes are a natural part of learning AI. Let's prepare you for some common issues and how to address them.

1. Syntax Errors

➢ **What Happens:** Your code doesn't run because of typos or incorrect formatting.
➢ **How to Fix It:** Read the error message carefully — it usually points to the exact line where the problem occurred.

2. Library Installation Issues

➢ **What   Happens:**   Errors   like "ModuleNotFoundError" occur if a required library isn't installed.
➢ **How to Fix It:** Install the missing library using pip

```
pip install [library_name]
```

3. Memory Errors

➢ **What Happens:** Large datasets or models can overload your computer's memory.
➢ **How to Fix It:** Use Google Colab or process smaller chunks of data at a time.

4. Debugging Tips

➢ Print values of variables at different stages to see where things go wrong.
➢ Use online communities like Stack Overflow to find solutions to specific errors.

By setting up your AI workspace, you're taking an essential step toward becoming an AI creator. Whether you choose to work locally on your computer or use cloud-based tools like Google Colab, the environment you create will be the foundation of your projects. With your tools ready, your Python installed, and your projects organized, you're now equipped to start coding and exploring the limitless possibilities of AI. Let's continue to the next chapter to dive deeper into practical AI development!

Chapter 04

Your First AI Program

You've learned the basics, set up your AI workspace, and are now ready for one of the most exciting steps: building your first AI program! This chapter walks you through everything from understanding Python basics to creating, testing, and running a simple AI model. By the end, you'll not only have a functional AI program but also a sense of pride in what you've accomplished. Let's get started!

Understanding Code Basics: A Crash Course in Python for AI Beginners

If you're new to programming, don't worry! Python is beginner-friendly, and you only need a few key concepts to start building AI programs.

1. Variables and Data Types

Variables store information your program uses, like numbers, text, or lists.

Example

```
name = "AI Creator"  # A string

age = 10  # An integer

skills = ["Python", "Machine Learning"]  # A list

print(name, age, skills)
```

2. Loops and Conditional Statements

Loops and conditions let your program make decisions and repeat tasks.

➢ Example of a **loop**:

```
for skill in skills: print(f"Learning {skill}")
```

```
Example of a condition
```

```
if age > 5:

    print("You' re ready to learn AI!")
```

3. Functions

Functions are blocks of reusable code.

Example

```
def greet_user(name):

    return f"Hello, {name}! Welcome to AI."
```

```
print(greet_user("AI Creator"))
```

4. Libraries

Libraries are collections of pre-written code that make tasks easier. For AI, you'll use libraries like NumPy, Pandas, and TensorFlow.

➢ Importing a library:

```
import numpy as np

numbers = np.array([1, 2, 3])

print(numbers * 2)
```

These basics will be enough to follow along as we dive into building your first AI program.

The Concept of Training Data: How to Find and Prepare Datasets

Training data is the heart of any AI program — it's what your AI learns from. Let's explore how to find and prepare this data.

1. What Is Training Data?

Training data is a collection of examples that teach your AI model to recognize patterns. For example:

➤ For a model identifying cats, training data might include thousands of cat images.
➤ For a sentiment analysis model, it might include text labeled as positive or negative.

2. Where to Find Datasets

➤ **Kaggle:** Offers a variety of free datasets for AI beginners.
➤ **Google Dataset Search:** A search engine for publicly available datasets.
➤ **UCI Machine Learning Repository:** A well-known source for beginner-friendly datasets.

3. Preparing Your Dataset

Data must be cleaned and formatted before it can be used:

➤ **Remove Errors:** Fix or remove incomplete or incorrect data.
➤ **Normalize Data:** Scale values to a consistent range, like 0 to 1.
➤ **Split Data:** Divide your dataset into:

✓ **Training Set:** Used to teach the model (70–80%).
✓ **Testing Set:** Used to evaluate the model (20–30%).

4. Example Dataset

For this chapter, we'll use a simple dataset to predict whether a student will pass based on their study hours.

Building a Simple AI Model: Step-by-Step Instructions to Create a Basic Model

Let's create a basic machine learning model using Python and the scikit-learn library. This model will predict whether a student will pass based on their study hours.

1. Import Necessary Libraries

```
import numpy as np
import pandas as pd
from sklearn.model_selection import train_test_split
from sklearn.linear_model import LogisticRegression
```

2. Create a Dataset

We'll simulate a small dataset for simplicity

```
# Sample data: hours studied and whether the student
passed (1 = Yes, 0 = No)
data = {
    "hours_studied": [1, 2, 3, 4, 5, 6, 7, 8, 9],
    "passed": [0, 0, 0, 1, 1, 1, 1, 1, 1]
}
df = pd.DataFrame(data)
```

3. Split the Dataset

Separate the dataset into training and testing sets

```
X = df[["hours_studied"]]  # Input (features)
y = df["passed"]  # Output (label)
X_train, X_test, y_train, y_test = train_test_split(X, y,
test_size=0.2, random_state=42)
```

4. Train the Model

Use logistic regression to create a simple AI model.

```
model = LogisticRegression()
model.fit(X_train, y_train)
```

Testing Your AI: How to Measure and Improve Your Program's Performance

Testing is crucial to ensure your model works well on new data.

1. Make Predictions on Test Data

```
predictions = model.predict(X_test)
print("Predictions:", predictions)
```

2. Measure Accuracy

Scikit-learn provides tools to measure model performance

```
from sklearn.metrics import accuracy_score
accuracy = accuracy_score(y_test, predictions)
print("Model Accuracy:", accuracy)
```

3. Improving the Model

If accuracy is low, consider:

➢ Collecting more data.
➢ Using a more complex model (like decision trees or neural networks).
➢ Fine-tuning hyperparameters (model settings).

Making Predictions: Running Your AI to See It in Action

Let's use your model to predict whether a student studying 6 hours will pass

```
# Predict for a new student
new_student = [[6]]
prediction = model.predict(new_student)
print("Will the student pass?", "Yes" if prediction[0] == 1 else "No")
```

Output

➢ **Input:** Hours studied = 6.
➢ **Prediction:** Yes (the student will pass).

Seeing your AI make real-world predictions is one of the most rewarding parts of this journey!

Celebrating Your Success: Reflecting on What You've Accomplished

Congratulations! You've built and tested your first AI program. Here's what you've achieved:

1. Learned Key Concepts

- Python basics.
- The importance of training data.
- How to test and measure an AI model.

2. Created an AI Model

You built a machine learning model that makes predictions based on data.

3. Took a Big Step Toward Becoming an AI Creator

This is just the beginning. With the skills you've learned, you can now explore more complex models, larger datasets, and advanced AI techniques.

Take a moment to celebrate your progress—you've earned it! Next, we'll dive deeper into building smarter AI programs in the upcoming chapters. Let's keep the momentum going!

Part 3: Diving Deeper Into AI Concepts

Chapter 05

How Machines Learns

Welcome to the next stage of your AI journey —
understanding *how* machines learn. While we've built a
basic AI model already, this chapter dives deeper into
the concepts behind machine learning (ML). You'll
explore how data and algorithms come together to
enable machines to make predictions and decisions. By
the end, you'll not only know how machines learn but
also understand how to evaluate their performance and
identify real-world applications for ML.

What Is Machine Learning? Real-Life Examples to Make It Clear

Machine learning is a subset of AI that enables
computers to learn and improve from experience
without being explicitly programmed. Instead of hard-
coding rules, we feed data into an algorithm, allowing
the machine to "learn" patterns and make predictions.

1. Simplified Definition

Machine learning is like teaching a computer using
examples instead of instructions. For instance:

➤ Teaching a computer to recognize spam emails by
showing it examples of spam and non-spam emails.

2. Key Real-Life Examples

➤ **Email Filters:** Gmail uses ML to classify emails
into Primary, Promotions, and Spam folders.
➤ **Streaming Services:** Netflix and Spotify
recommend shows or music based on your past
activity.

> **Health Monitoring:** Smartwatches detect irregular heartbeats or other health conditions using ML.
> **Self-Driving Cars:** Autonomous vehicles use ML to interpret sensor data and make driving decisions.

3. Why ML Matters

Unlike traditional programming, ML systems improve over time as they receive more data, making them ideal for solving problems that are too complex for manual coding.

Supervised vs. Unsupervised Learning: Key Differences and Use Cases

Machine learning can be categorized into two main types: supervised and unsupervised learning. Understanding these distinctions will help you decide which approach to use for your projects.

1. Supervised Learning

> **How It Works:** The algorithm learns from labeled data (data with known outputs).

✓ Example: Predicting housing prices based on labeled data, such as square footage and price.

• **Use Cases:**

> Predicting stock prices.
> Diagnosing diseases from medical images.

> Classifying emails as spam or not spam.

2. Unsupervised Learning

> **How It Works:** The algorithm learns from unlabeled data and identifies patterns or groupings on its own.

✓ Example: Grouping customers based on purchasing behavior.

> **Use Cases:**

✓ Customer segmentation for marketing.
✓ Anomaly detection in network security.
✓ Recommender systems (e.g., "Customers who bought this also bought...").

3. Key Differences

Aspect	Supervised Learning	Unsupervised Learning
Data	Labeled (with outputs)	Unlabeled (no outputs)
Goal	Make predictions or classifications	Discover hidden patterns
Examples	Predicting house prices	Clustering customers by behavior

Training Models: What Happens Behind the Scenes When Machines Learn

When you "train" a machine learning model, several things happen behind the scenes. Let's break it down:

1. Input and Output

➤ **Input (Features):** The variables the model uses to make predictions (e.g., square footage of a house).
➤ **Output (Label):** The value the model is trying to predict (e.g., house price).

2. Steps in Training

➤ **Step 1: Initialization:** The model starts with random values for parameters (like weights in a neural network).
➤ **Step 2: Learning:** The model adjusts its parameters to minimize error by comparing predictions with actual labels.
➤ **Step 3: Iteration:** This process is repeated until the model improves enough or meets a predefined condition.

3. The Role of Algorithms

➤ Algorithms like Linear Regression or Decision Trees define *how* the model learns from data.
➤ The choice of algorithm depends on the problem type and data structure.

Evaluating Your AI Model: Metrics Like Accuracy, Precision, and Recall

After training a model, the next step is to evaluate its performance. Here's how to measure how well your AI is performing:

1. Key Metrics

➢ **Accuracy:** The percentage of correct predictions.

- Example: If your model makes 90 correct predictions out of 100, accuracy is 90%.

➢ **Precision:** How many of the positive predictions were correct.

- Example: Out of 50 emails predicted as spam, 45 were actually spam (precision = 90%).

➢ **Recall:** How many of the actual positives were correctly identified.

- Example: Out of 100 spam emails, your model identified 80 (recall = 80%).

2. Confusion Matrix

A confusion matrix breaks down the performance of a classification model into:

➢ **True Positives (TP):** Correctly predicted positives.

➢ **True Negatives (TN):** Correctly predicted negatives.

> **False Positives (FP):** Predicted positive but actually negative.
> **False Negatives (FN):** Predicted negative but actually positive.

	Predicted Positive	Predicted Negative
Actual Positive	True Positive (TP)	False Negative (FN)
Actual Negative	False Positive (FP)	True Negative (TN)

The Role of Neural Networks: An Introduction to Deep Learning

Neural networks power some of the most advanced AI applications today, from facial recognition to voice assistants. Here's a beginner-friendly explanation:

1. What Are Neural Networks?

Neural networks are algorithms inspired by the human brain. They consist of:

> **Input Layer:** Receives data.
> **Hidden Layers:** Process data through mathematical operations.
> **Output Layer:** Produces the result (e.g., classification or prediction).

2. How They Work

- ➢ Each "neuron" in a layer takes input, applies a mathematical function, and passes the result to the next layer.
- ➢ The network adjusts weights during training to improve accuracy.

3. Applications

- ➢ **Image Recognition:** Identifying objects in photos.
- ➢ **Speech-to-Text:** Converting spoken words into text.
- ➢ **Game AI:** Beating human players in chess or Go.

Practical Applications: Identifying Projects Where ML Makes Sense

Now that you understand how machines learn, let's explore how to identify problems that machine learning can solve effectively.

1. Characteristics of Good ML Projects

- ➢ **Lots of Data:** Machine learning thrives on large datasets.
- ➢ **Clear Goals:** The problem should have measurable outcomes (e.g., predict sales).
- ➢ **Complex Patterns:** Problems that are too complex for manual coding.

2. Examples of Practical Applications

- ➢ **Predictive Analytics:** Forecasting sales or customer demand.

> **Personalization:** Tailoring recommendations on e-commerce sites.
> **Automation:** Streamlining repetitive tasks like document classification.

3. Brainstorm Your Own Ideas

> Look around your daily life or workplace for tasks involving repetitive decisions or predictions.
> Ask yourself: "Could an algorithm handle this task more efficiently?"

Understanding how machines learn is a game-changer in your AI journey. You've now explored machine learning types, how models are trained, and how to evaluate their success. With this knowledge, you're ready to take on more sophisticated AI projects. Next, we'll deepen your understanding by exploring how AI handles more complex datasets and builds smarter models. Let's keep going!

Chapter 06

AI in the Real World

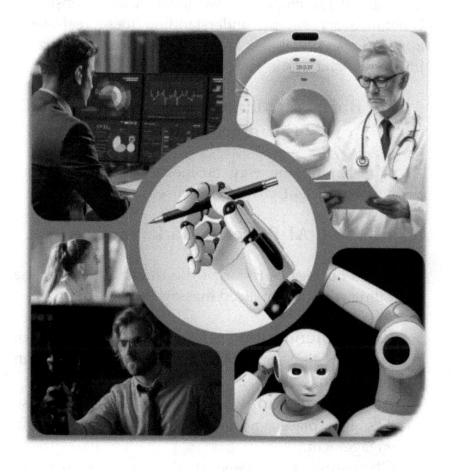

Artificial intelligence has moved far beyond the realm of research labs and into our everyday lives. In this chapter, we'll explore how AI is transforming industries like business, medicine, education, and entertainment. You'll also discover how AI is being used for social good and learn about the challenges we must tackle to ensure it benefits everyone. By understanding these real-world applications, you'll see the potential of AI to create impactful solutions in your own projects.

AI in Business: Marketing, Automation, and Customer Insights

AI is reshaping the way businesses operate, making them more efficient, customer-focused, and data-driven.

1. AI-Powered Marketing

AI allows businesses to target the right audience at the right time with personalized messages.

> **Recommendation Engines:** E-commerce platforms like Amazon suggest products based on past purchases.
> **Ad Optimization:** Google Ads and Facebook use AI to place ads strategically, maximizing engagement.
> **Chatbots:** AI-powered chatbots answer customer queries 24/7, improving customer satisfaction and saving costs.

2. Business Process Automation

Repetitive, manual tasks are being automated, freeing up employees to focus on higher-value work.

> **Invoice Processing:** AI extracts data from invoices, reducing errors.
> **HR Recruitment:** Tools like LinkedIn AI match candidates to job descriptions.
> **Supply Chain Optimization:** AI predicts demand and automates inventory management.

3. Customer Insights

AI analyzes vast amounts of data to help businesses understand their customers better.

> **Sentiment Analysis:** AI tools analyze social media posts to gauge customer opinions.
> **Predictive Analytics:** Businesses forecast trends and customer behavior using AI.
> **CRM Systems:** AI-powered customer relationship management (CRM) platforms, like Salesforce Einstein, recommend next steps for nurturing leads.

AI in Medicine: Diagnostics, Drug Discovery, and Personalized Treatments

The healthcare industry has been revolutionized by AI, making diagnostics faster, treatments more precise, and drug discovery more efficient.

1. Diagnostic Accuracy

AI is enhancing the speed and accuracy of diagnosing diseases:

➤ **Medical Imaging:** AI systems like Google's DeepMind can detect eye diseases and cancer in X-rays and MRIs with remarkable precision.
➤ **Early Disease Detection:** Tools like IBM Watson analyze patient records and flag potential health issues.

2. Drug Discovery

Developing new drugs is a time-consuming and expensive process, but AI is accelerating it:

➤ AI models simulate how drugs interact with the human body, reducing the need for lengthy trials.
➤ Companies like Insilico Medicine use AI to identify new drug candidates in weeks instead of years.

3. Personalized Medicine

AI enables treatments tailored to individual patients:

➤ **Genomic Analysis:** AI analyzes genetic data to recommend specific therapies.
➤ **Predictive Models:** AI predicts how a patient might respond to treatment based on their medical history.
➤ **Wearables:** Devices like Fitbit and Apple Watch monitor real-time health data, helping doctors intervene early.

AI in Education: Personalized Learning and Intelligent Tutoring Systems

AI is transforming education by making learning more accessible, personalized, and engaging.

1. Adaptive Learning Platforms

AI-powered tools like Khan Academy and Coursera adapt to each student's learning pace:

➢ Students struggling with a concept receive additional exercises.
➢ Advanced learners are provided with challenging content.

2. Intelligent Tutoring Systems

AI acts as a personal tutor, providing instant feedback and guidance.

➢ Examples include platforms like Carnegie Learning and Duolingo, which use AI to correct mistakes and suggest improvements.

3. Accessibility and Inclusion

AI enables students with disabilities to access education more effectively:

➢ **Text-to-Speech:** Tools like Microsoft's Seeing AI help visually impaired students.

> **Speech Recognition:** AI converts spoken language into text, assisting students with hearing impairments.

4. Streamlining Administrative Tasks

AI automates tasks like grading, scheduling, and managing class records, giving teachers more time to focus on students.

AI in Entertainment: How Netflix and Spotify Recommend Content

Entertainment platforms are leveraging AI to keep users engaged and satisfied.

1. Personalized Recommendations

Netflix and Spotify analyze user behavior to suggest content they're likely to enjoy:

> **Netflix:** Tracks viewing habits, genres, and ratings to recommend movies and shows.
> **Spotify:** Analyzes listening habits to create personalized playlists like "Discover Weekly."

2. Content Creation

AI is even creating content:

> **Music Composition:** AI tools like Amper Music and AIVA compose background scores.

> **Video Game Design:** AI generates game environments and non-player character behavior.

3. Enhanced Viewing Experiences

> **Live Streaming:** AI adjusts video quality based on your internet speed.
> **Subtitles and Dubbing:** AI generates subtitles and dubs in multiple languages.

AI for Good: Fighting Climate Change, Poverty, and Inequality

AI is being used to address some of humanity's most pressing challenges.

1. Tackling Climate Change

> **Energy Optimization:** AI predicts energy usage patterns to reduce waste.
> **Environmental Monitoring:** Tools like Global Forest Watch use AI to monitor deforestation.
> **Sustainable Agriculture:** AI-powered drones analyze soil quality and monitor crop health.

2. Alleviating Poverty

> **Resource Allocation:** AI helps NGOs distribute food and supplies more efficiently.
> **Education Access:** AI-powered apps provide free learning resources to underserved communities.

3. Reducing Inequality

➤ **Job Matching:** AI platforms connect job seekers with opportunities based on skills, reducing unemployment.
➤ **Healthcare Access:** Telemedicine platforms powered by AI bring medical advice to remote areas.

Challenges to Solve: Bias, Misinformation, and Transparency

Despite its benefits, AI is not without challenges. Addressing these issues is crucial for ensuring AI serves humanity equitably.

1. Bias in AI Models

➤ AI systems can inherit biases from their training data, leading to unfair outcomes (e.g., biased hiring algorithms).
➤ To mitigate this, diverse datasets and transparency in model design are essential.

2. Spread of Misinformation

➤ AI-generated content, such as deepfakes, can spread false information.
➤ Tools like deepfake detectors and fact-checking algorithms are being developed to counteract this.

3. Lack of Transparency

➤ Many AI systems are "black boxes," making it difficult to understand their decision-making process.
➤ Researchers are working on "explainable AI" to make models more interpretable.

4. Privacy Concerns

➤ AI often relies on personal data, raising questions about privacy.
➤ Regulations like GDPR aim to ensure responsible data use.

AI is already changing the world in profound ways, and its potential to solve real-world problems is immense. Whether it's enhancing business efficiency, transforming healthcare, personalizing education, or addressing global challenges, the opportunities are endless. However, as creators and users of AI, we must also remain mindful of the ethical and societal implications. By understanding these real-world applications and challenges, you are better equipped to use AI responsibly and innovatively.

Part 4
Becoming an AI Creator

Chapter 07

Exploring AI Projects for Beginners

Congratulations on making it this far! By now, you've built a foundational understanding of artificial intelligence and how it works. It's time to take the leap from theory to practice by diving into beginner-friendly AI projects. In this chapter, you'll learn how to approach four hands-on projects, discover where to find inspiration for your own ideas, and understand the importance of documenting your work to showcase your skills. Let's get started on your journey to becoming an AI creator!

Project 1: Predicting House Prices – Building a Simple Regression Model

One of the simplest and most practical applications of AI is predicting numerical values using regression models. Let's create a project to predict house prices based on features like size, location, and number of rooms.

Step 1: Understanding the Problem

The goal is to predict the price of a house given certain features. This is a classic example of supervised learning, specifically regression.

Step 2: Collecting and Preparing the Data

➤ **Dataset:** Use publicly available datasets like the **Kaggle Housing Price Dataset**.
➤ **Data Features:** Include features such as square footage, number of bedrooms, location, and age of the house.

> **Data Cleaning:** Handle missing values, remove duplicates, and normalize numerical data.

Step 3: Creating the Model

> Use **Linear Regression** as your model for simplicity.
> Split your dataset into **training** and **testing** subsets.
> Train the model on the training data to find relationships between house features and their prices.

Step 4: Evaluating Performance

> Use metrics like **Mean Absolute Error (MAE)** or **Root Mean Square Error (RMSE)** to measure accuracy.
> Test the model on unseen data to check its ability to generalize.

Step 5: Making Predictions

Input sample data (e.g., a 1,200-square-foot house with 3 bedrooms) and let the model predict its price.

Project 2: Image Recognition – Training an AI to Identify Objects

Image recognition is one of the most exciting applications of AI. In this project, we'll build a simple model to classify images of objects, such as cats and dogs.

Step 1: Understanding the Problem

The goal is to train an AI to recognize and classify images based on their content.

Step 2: Collecting and Preparing the Data

- ➢ **Dataset:** Use datasets like the **CIFAR-10** or **Dogs vs. Cats** dataset from Kaggle.
- ➢ **Data Augmentation:** Enhance your training data by flipping, rotating, or cropping images to improve the model's robustness.

Step 3: Creating the Model

- ➢ Use a pre-built AI framework like **TensorFlow** or **PyTorch**.
- ➢ Build a **Convolutional Neural Network (CNN)**, as it's well-suited for image recognition tasks.
- ➢ Include layers for convolution, pooling, and fully connected operations.

Step 4: Training and Testing

- ➢ Train the CNN on labeled images of cats and dogs.
- ➢ Evaluate performance using metrics like **accuracy** and **F1-score**.

Step 5: Making Predictions

Upload an image to the trained model and watch as it correctly classifies the object (e.g., "This is a dog!").

Project 3: Sentiment Analysis – Teaching AI to Read and Analyze Text

Sentiment analysis is the process of teaching AI to identify emotions and opinions in text. For this project, we'll analyze whether customer reviews are positive or negative.

Step 1: Understanding the Problem

The objective is to classify text (e.g., reviews) as positive, neutral, or negative.

Step 2: Collecting and Preparing the Data

➢ **Dataset:** Use datasets like the **IMDB Movie Reviews Dataset** or Twitter sentiment data.
➢ **Preprocessing:**

✓ Remove unnecessary characters, stop words (e.g., "the," "and"), and punctuation.
✓ Tokenize the text into words.
✓ Convert words into numerical representations using tools like **Word2Vec** or **TF-IDF**.

Step 3: Creating the Model

➢ Use a **Recurrent Neural Network (RNN)** or simpler algorithms like **Naive Bayes**.
➢ Train the model on labeled datasets, where each text sample is tagged as positive or negative.

Step 4: Evaluating Performance

- ➤ Use metrics such as **precision, recall,** and **accuracy** to evaluate how well your model performs.

Step 5: Making Predictions

Input a customer review (e.g., "The product is fantastic!") and let the AI classify it as positive or negative.

Project 4: Chatbot Creation – Developing a Basic Conversational Bot

Chatbots are one of the most widely used applications of AI. In this project, you'll build a simple bot that can answer user questions.

Step 1: Understanding the Problem

The goal is to create a conversational agent that responds intelligently to user inputs.

Step 2: Setting Up the Framework

- ➤ Use **Python** libraries like **NLTK, SpaCy,** or **Rasa** to build your chatbot.
- ➤ Decide the type of bot:

- ✓ **Rule-Based Bot:** Simple pre-defined responses.
- ✓ **AI-Powered Bot:** Learns from conversations using **Natural Language Processing (NLP).**

Step 3: Defining Intent and Responses

> Create a set of **intents** (e.g., greetings, FAQs) and link them to appropriate responses.

Example:

✓ **User:** "Hello!"
✓ **Bot:** "Hi there! How can I assist you today?"

Step 4: Training the Bot

> Train the chatbot on sample conversations or datasets like **Cornell Movie-Dialogs Corpus**.

Step 5: Testing and Deployment

> Test the chatbot with various inputs to ensure it responds accurately.
> Deploy it on a messaging platform like WhatsApp or Telegram.

How to Find Ideas: Sources of Inspiration for More AI Projects

Once you've completed these beginner projects, the next step is to brainstorm your own ideas. Here's how to get started:

1. Look at Everyday Problems

> Think about repetitive tasks you perform daily that could be automated.
> Example: AI to track grocery inventory and suggest shopping lists.

2. Browse Online Communities

➤ Platforms like Kaggle, GitHub, and Reddit's r/MachineLearning offer project ideas and datasets.

3. Leverage Your Interests

➤ Combine AI with your hobbies, such as music composition, fitness tracking, or photography.

4. Solve Real-World Challenges

➤ Consider broader societal issues like climate change, healthcare access, or education.

Documenting Your Work: Creating Portfolios to Showcase Your Skills

Building projects is just the first step. Documenting and presenting them effectively is essential to demonstrate your skills to others.

1. Create a Portfolio Website

➤ Use platforms like **GitHub Pages**, **WordPress**, or **Notion** to host your portfolio.

2. Include Detailed Case Studies

For each project, include:

➤ **Problem Statement:** What you set out to achieve.

- ➢ **Methodology:** The tools, frameworks, and data you used.
- ➢ **Results:** Metrics and examples of predictions.
- ➢ **Challenges:** Problems you faced and how you solved them.

3. Share on Social Platforms

- ➢ Post your projects on LinkedIn, Twitter, or AI forums to gain visibility and feedback.

4. Collaborate and Learn

- ➢ Open-source your projects on GitHub to collaborate with others and receive constructive criticism.

By diving into these projects, you'll not only solidify your AI skills but also build a portfolio that demonstrates your abilities to others. Each project is an opportunity to learn something new, solve real-world problems, and showcase your creativity. You're well on your way to becoming an AI creator—let's keep building!

Chapter 08

Building Your AI Skills for the Future

You've taken your first steps into the world of artificial intelligence, and now it's time to think about the road ahead. AI is a fast-evolving field with endless opportunities for growth, exploration, and impact. Whether you're aiming for a career in AI or simply want to deepen your understanding, this chapter will guide you through actionable steps to build your skills, expand your knowledge, and position yourself for success.

Expanding Your Learning: Free Courses, Books, and Communities

The key to building a strong foundation in AI is consistent learning. Fortunately, there's no shortage of accessible resources.

1. Free Online Courses

Many high-quality courses are available online for free:

- **Coursera**: Andrew Ng's "Machine Learning" course is a classic starting point.
- **edX**: Offers free courses like "Artificial Intelligence for Everyone" from top universities.
- **Google AI**: Their "Machine Learning Crash Course" is beginner-friendly and practical.
- **Kaggle Learn**: Bite-sized lessons on Python, machine learning, and more.

2. Books for AI Beginners

Books provide in-depth learning and long-term reference material:

- ➤ **"Artificial Intelligence: A Guide to Intelligent Systems" by Michael Negnevitsky**: A beginner-friendly introduction to AI concepts.
- ➤ **"Python Machine Learning" by Sebastian Raschka**: Great for hands-on projects.
- ➤ **"Deep Learning for Beginners" by Dr. Samuel Burns**: Explains neural networks in simple terms.

3. Learn by Doing

- ➤ Participate in online coding challenges like **Kaggle Competitions** and **HackerRank AI problems**.
- ➤ Explore datasets on **UCI Machine Learning Repository** or **Google Dataset Search** for practice.

Joining AI Communities: Forums, Meetups, and Online Groups to Network

The AI field thrives on collaboration and the exchange of ideas. By engaging with communities, you'll gain access to insights, mentorship, and networking opportunities.

1. Online Communities

- ➤ **Reddit**: Join subreddits like r/MachineLearning, r/learnprogramming, and r/datascience for advice and discussions.
- ➤ **Stack Overflow**: Ask questions and share solutions with a global community of AI enthusiasts.

> **LinkedIn Groups**: Follow industry leaders and participate in discussions in groups like "Artificial Intelligence and Machine Learning."

2. Local AI Meetups

> Use platforms like **Meetup.com** to find AI-related events and workshops in your area.
> Attend hackathons to collaborate on projects with others and learn in a team setting.

3. Online Events and Webinars

> Platforms like **Eventbrite** and **AI for Good** host free webinars featuring experts and researchers in AI.
> Join live coding sessions or Q&A events to deepen your practical understanding.

4. Networking Tips

> Don't be afraid to ask questions; AI communities are often welcoming to beginners.
> Build a network of peers and mentors who can guide your learning and career.

Contributing to Open Source: Why and How to Get Involved in Collaborative Projects

Open source projects are a fantastic way to sharpen your skills and gain real-world experience while giving back to the community.

1. Benefits of Open Source Contributions

- ➤ Gain hands-on experience working on real-world projects.
- ➤ Improve your problem-solving and coding skills.
- ➤ Collaborate with developers from around the world and build your network.

2. Finding Projects to Contribute To

- ➤ Explore GitHub repositories related to AI, like **scikit-learn**, **TensorFlow**, or **OpenCV**.
- ➤ Start with beginner-friendly projects labeled **"good first issue"** or **"help wanted."**

3. How to Get Started

- ➤ Fork the repository and familiarize yourself with the codebase.
- ➤ Read the contribution guidelines carefully.
- ➤ Start small—fix bugs, improve documentation, or write test cases.

4. Tools to Simplify Collaboration

- ➤ Use **Git** for version control.
- ➤ Communicate with project maintainers via GitHub discussions or Slack channels.

Experimenting with Advanced Tools: Diving into NLP, CV, and Generative AI

Once you've mastered the basics, it's time to explore advanced AI domains and tools that are shaping the future.

1. Natural Language Processing (NLP)

➤ NLP focuses on teaching machines to understand and generate human language.
➤ Tools to explore:

✓ **NLTK** and **spaCy** for text processing.
✓ **Hugging Face Transformers** for pre-trained models like BERT and GPT.

2. Computer Vision (CV)

➤ CV enables machines to interpret visual data like images and videos.
➤ Tools to explore:

✓ **OpenCV** for image processing.
✓ **YOLO (You Only Look Once)** for object detection.
✓ **Keras** for creating convolutional neural networks (CNNs).

3. Generative AI

➤ Generative AI focuses on creating new content, such as text, images, and music.
➤ Tools to explore:
➤ **DALL·E** and **Stable Diffusion** for image generation.
➤ **GPT-based models** for text generation.

AI Certifications: Which Ones Are Worth Pursuing and Why

Certifications can validate your skills and enhance your credibility as an AI professional.

1. Top AI Certifications

➢ **Google Professional Machine Learning Engineer**: Focuses on deploying ML models in production.
➢ **Microsoft Azure AI Engineer Associate**: For those interested in AI on Azure's cloud platform.
➢ **IBM AI Engineering Professional Certificate**: A beginner-friendly option that includes practical projects.
➢ **AWS Certified Machine Learning – Specialty**: Ideal for cloud-based AI applications.

2. Benefits of Certifications

➢ Showcase your expertise to potential employers.
➢ Gain structured learning through certification courses.
➢ Stand out in a competitive job market.

3. Choosing the Right Certification

➢ Consider your career goals. For example, cloud-based certifications are ideal for those aiming to work with AI infrastructure.
➢ Look for certifications that include hands-on projects or real-world case studies.

Planning Your AI Career: Opportunities in Development, Research, and Entrepreneurship

AI offers diverse career paths, whether you're interested in building systems, conducting research, or launching your own venture.

1. Career Paths in AI

➤ **AI Developer**: Build and deploy AI applications and models.
➤ **Data Scientist**: Focus on analyzing and interpreting complex data.
➤ **AI Researcher**: Advance the field by creating new algorithms and theories.
➤ **AI Product Manager**: Oversee AI-driven products from concept to deployment.
➤ **AI Entrepreneur**: Start your own business using AI to solve real-world problems.

2. Essential Skills for AI Careers

➤ Strong programming skills (e.g., Python, R, or Java).
➤ Knowledge of AI frameworks like TensorFlow or PyTorch.
➤ Problem-solving and critical thinking abilities.

3. Finding Job Opportunities

➤ Use platforms like **LinkedIn**, **AngelList**, and **Glassdoor** to find AI-related roles.

> Participate in hackathons and competitions to gain visibility.

4. Starting Your AI Business

> Identify a problem that AI can solve efficiently.
> Build a prototype and test it with potential users.
> Seek funding from venture capitalists or AI innovation grants.

Final Thoughts

AI is an exciting and dynamic field with endless opportunities to learn, grow, and make a difference. By expanding your skills, joining communities, contributing to open source, and exploring advanced tools, you'll be well-equipped to thrive in the world of AI. Whether you choose a career path in development, research, or entrepreneurship, the future is bright for AI creators like you. Keep learning, stay curious, and let your creativity guide you toward success!

Conclusion

Your Journey as an AI Creator

As you close this book, take a moment to celebrate how far you've come. Whether you've followed every chapter step-by-step or jumped to the sections that piqued your interest, you've taken meaningful steps toward understanding and creating with artificial intelligence. This isn't just the end of a book—it's the beginning of your journey as an AI creator.

Reflecting on Your Progress: Celebrate What You've Learned and Built

Think back to where you started.

➢ You began with no knowledge of AI, yet now you can explain key concepts, build simple models, and even apply AI to real-world problems.
➢ Remember your first program? Whether it was a simple prediction model or a small chatbot, that was your gateway into a vast and exciting field.

Take pride in what you've achieved:

➢ **Concept Mastery**: You now understand what AI is and why it matters.
➢ **Hands-on Skills**: You've set up an AI workspace, built projects, and explored tools like TensorFlow and scikit-learn.
➢ **Confidence**: You've overcome the initial intimidation of AI and proven that anyone, regardless of background, can learn to create with AI.

Reflect on how much you've grown—not just in knowledge, but in your ability to tackle new challenges.

The Future of AI and You: Staying Informed About AI Trends

The world of AI is constantly evolving, and staying up-to-date is crucial for growth. Here's how to ensure you remain informed and relevant:

1. Follow AI News and Updates

➢ Subscribe to newsletters like **Towards Data Science** or **AI Weekly**.
➢ Read trusted publications like **MIT Technology Review**, **Wired**, or **The Verge** for AI advancements.

2. Watch for Breakthroughs in Key Areas

➢ **Generative AI**: Tools like ChatGPT and DALL·E are just the beginning—stay tuned for what's next.
➢ **Edge AI**: The shift from cloud to on-device AI is growing rapidly.
➢ **AI Ethics**: Monitor developments in fairness, accountability, and regulation to stay responsible in your work.

3. Network with Experts and Innovators

Attend AI conferences such as **NeurIPS**, **ICLR**, or regional meetups. Even virtual attendance can expose you to cutting-edge ideas.

4. Follow Key Thought Leaders

On platforms like Twitter or LinkedIn, follow AI researchers, developers, and entrepreneurs who share insights about the field.

Resources for Continued Growth: Recommended Websites, Books, and Mentors

As you progress, you'll need deeper resources to keep learning and growing.

1. Websites and Online Platforms

- ➢ **Coursera** and **edX**: Advanced courses like "Deep Learning Specialization" by Andrew Ng.
- ➢ **Kaggle**: Continue participating in competitions to refine your skills.
- ➢ **GitHub**: Follow popular AI repositories to study advanced implementations.

2. Books for Advanced Learning

- ➢ **"Deep Learning" by Ian Goodfellow**: A foundational text for understanding neural networks and deep learning.
- ➢ **"Hands-On Machine Learning with Scikit-Learn, Keras, and TensorFlow" by Aurélien Géron**: A practical guide for intermediate learners.
- ➢ **"Life 3.0" by Max Tegmark**: Explore the societal impact of AI and its future potential.

3. Finding Mentors

➢ Join communities like **AI4ALL**, which connect beginners with mentors in AI.
➢ Network at local meetups or online forums to find experienced professionals willing to guide you.

Encouragement to Keep Creating: Embrace Mistakes as Learning Opportunities

AI development is not a straight path—it's full of challenges, failures, and unexpected outcomes. Here's why that's a good thing:

➢ **Mistakes Are Lessons**: Every error in your code or unexpected model behavior teaches you something new. Embrace these moments as essential to your learning process.
➢ **Persistence Pays Off**: Many of the greatest AI breakthroughs happened after countless failures. Your journey is no different.
➢ **Creativity Thrives on Iteration**: The more you experiment, the better you'll understand what works and what doesn't.

Tips for Staying Motivated

➢ Break larger projects into smaller, achievable milestones.
➢ Celebrate small wins, like successfully debugging an issue or improving a model's accuracy.
➢ Revisit old projects to see how much you've improved over time.

Remember, every AI expert was once a beginner. What sets them apart is their persistence and willingness to learn from every setback.

Closing Words: You're Now Part of the AI Revolution

By completing this book, you've joined a community of innovators shaping the future with artificial intelligence. AI isn't just about machines; it's about human creativity, problem-solving, and making the world a better place.

A Call to Action

- Don't stop here—keep exploring, building, and dreaming. The more you create, the more confident you'll become.
- Share your projects with others. Whether it's through online forums, social media, or your local community, your work can inspire others to embark on their own AI journey.

Remember This

AI is a tool, and you are the creator. With curiosity, passion, and hard work, there's no limit to what you can achieve.

The AI revolution is just beginning, and you are now a part of it. So go forth, push boundaries, and keep creating. The future is in your hands.

Thank you for trusting this guide to kickstart your journey. Your adventure in AI is only just beginning!